TO
Grandma

1982

Y0-BGG-308

Love
Autumn & Laurie

A Grandmother Is For Loving

Selected by Stephanie C. Oda

THE C.R.GIBSON COMPANY
Norwalk, Connecticut

Because this page cannot accommodate all the copyright notices, the section in the back of the book designated ''Acknowledgments'' constitutes an extension of the copyright page.

Copyright © MCMLXXXI by
The C.R. Gibson Company
All rights reserved
Printed in the United States of America
ISBN: 0-8378-1710-2

What Is a Grandmother?

A Grandmother—bless her—
Is a number of things,
There's no end to the joy
That a Grandmother brings!

She's receptive and loving,
And so understanding,
She teaches and guides you
As your world is expanding;

She's never too busy
To be generous and giving
Of her talent, her time,
And her wisdom in living;

A Grandmother's someone
Who will back up your schemes,
And encourage your plans,
Your hopes and your dreams;

She's a little bit Mother,
A little bit friend,
Someone on whom
You can always depend...
Someone in your life
Who plays a big part,
Someone who loves you
With all of her heart!

Katherine Nelson Davis

The Many Styles of Grandparents

Your status as a grandparent doesn't mean that your days of dancing, skating, bowling, taking safaris or wearing pant-suits are over. In fact, in a recent Broadway play, the seventeen-year-old granddaughter accuses her middle-aged grandmother of having filched her red tights. If you happen to have a fourth generation member living in the family, that great grandparent, you may still consider him or her as the grandparent.

Grandparents come in a variety of types. There are those who look or act like the traditional story-book types and there are those who defy any typing. There are many grandmothers who have the time and leisure to relieve their daughters and daughters-in-law—as well as relive their own early mothering days—as they offer to give a hand with the babies. This time 'round they expect to notice, in slow motion, all those many little changes and steps in their grandchild's development that they were too busy to notice in their own children during those harried and hurried early mothering years. They hope to relish the youngsters with more delight—and of course you can always go home for a good night's sleep!

There are others—and you aren't a cold, remote, un-feeling grandparent if you happen to be among this group—who prefer to skip this round, thank you. They did their best with their own brood and don't want to go in heavily for baby-sitting and all it involves. The prospect of changing diapers may not send you, and the mere idea of keeping an eye on or chasing toddlers just exhausts you. Many such grandparents enjoy the youngsters more when they are older and offer other kinds of cooperation to their young families.

Still others, often working grandmothers, have lives that are so busy and full that they aren't able to devote much time to the youngest generation. For these families, it is sometimes the fourth generation, active and spry in their sixties and seventies who stand in for the third generation!

Helene S. Arnstein

About Children

By all the published facts in the case,
Children belong to the human race.

Equipped with consciousness, passions, pulse,
They even grow up and become adults.

So why's the resemblance, moral or mental,
Of children to people so coincidental?

Upright out of primordial dens,
Homo walked and was sapiens.

But rare as leviathans or auks
Is—male or female—the child who walks.

He runs, he gallops, he crawls, he pounces,
Flies, leaps, stands on his head, or bounces,

Imitates snakes or the tiger striped
But seldom recalls he is labeled "Biped."

Which man or woman have you set sights on
Who craves to slumber with all the lights on

Yet creeps away to a lampless nook
In order to pore on a comic book?

Why, if (according to A. Gesell)
The minds of children ring clear as a bell,

Does every question one asks a tot
Receive the similar answer—"What?"

And who ever started the baseless rumor
That any child has a sense of humor?

Children conceive of no jest that's madder
Than Daddy falling from a ten-foot ladder.

Their fancies sway like jetsam and flotsam;
One minute they're winsome, the next they're swatsome.

While sweet their visages, soft their arts are,
Cold as a mermaiden's kiss their hearts are;

They comprehend neither pity nor treason.
An hour to them is a three months' season.

So who can say—this is just between us—
That children and we are a common genus,

When the selfsame nimbus is eerily worn
By a nymph, a child, and a unicorn?

Phyllis McGinley

Small Fortune

This year of sudden dividends
swelled an account for me
lately depleted; now it ends
fearful frugality.

I count my blessings without dread
of some potential loss
and savor the gold-ringleted
small fortune I possess.

Here in my son's wide-open house
Love is on constant loan:
I hold his children dear and close
as I once held my own.

Anne Marx

To My Grandson, Alexander
(Age—4 months)

I wonder what you're thinking about
as you follow me with your dark blue eyes,
as you look so wondering and wise,
as you smile your devastating smile—
What do you think about all the while?

I say to myself that a baby your age
can't possibly think—yet I haven't a doubt
that you're thinking of things to think about,
and dreaming of dreams the future will frame,
Dreams that will some day have a name.

Dorothy Joslin

"Wait For Me, Butterfly!"

The woman who lives exactly next door to me has an enchanting assortment of tiny grandchildren, all of whom look and behave as if they were friends of Charlie Brown. One Sunday morning I was driving to church and noticed a tow-headed infant (about two) running along the low wall that edges their property. The snappers in his corduroy overalls had become unsnapped and the legs of the pants were flapping out behind him. He was holding his fat little hands high in the air, reaching out, and he was calling something. I couldn't see any sign of a ball, but I slowed down to hear what he was saying. What he was saying was, "Wait for me, butterfly!"

Jean Kerr

The Pushover

My grandchild, who, when walking, wobbles,
Calls dogs Bow-wows, and turkeys, Gobbles.
Today I called a cow Moo-moo;
She's got me talking that way too.

Ogden Nash

A Child Ran Here

Scurrying down the trail ahead
My small grandchild runs, touching
Each flower passing, pausing now
To contemplate a monarch, folded still.
Anchored to the rocks, gulls flock
Like children at a game, crying
Shrieks for a clam prize.
Through the chestnut grove we pluck up
The burgeoning loot, to inspect.
Rippled mahogany, soft on the cheek,
Pearls, strung on colored yarn for
A carnival, perhaps another day.
They shriveled like old people,
Waning with the years.
How short the precious years
A child runs here.
Two of us, one graying, one small
Innocence, yet two children chase,
With autumn catching their breath, with
Bright colored fire, stones and pebbles
Caught in their shoes, flying over the sand,
Near the green water rushing the tide in,
Pulling down the clocks, caught in a
Photograph, to keep, a remembrance.

Elizabeth Revere

The Unplanned Visit

Sometimes an opportunity to have a grandchild alone presents itself unsought. In one family the younger grandchildren, two little girls, had quite naturally made themselves at home in grandmother's house, but the eldest, a boy, had drawn away to his own interests in the middle school years and the grandmother felt she scarcely knew him. Then one summer, just before he was to go to summer camp, he broke his arm. The family was to go away two weeks later, but here were two weeks when the boy's friends were all away and he would have nothing to do. Seeing him disappointed and disconsolate, grandmother asked if he would like to visit her and his grandfather at their cottage in the country.

Those two weeks were memorable for all three. The grandparents discovered their grandson and the grandson discovered his grandparents. There were other boys his age in the neighborhood, but although he was friendly he did not seek their company. He preferred to work beside grandmother—one-armed, to be sure—in the garden, or with grandfather who was repairing the porch. He shared their early morning and twilight strolls. They had known him as rather a silent boy when the whole family was together, but after the first uneasy day of being alone with them he began opening up, and for two weeks they never had a moment's pause in finding something to talk about together.

Ruth Goode

The Little Monarch

I am a willing captive of this Prince,
marshmallow soft on padded high-chaired throne—
who waves a silver scepter through his bowl
emptied of milk and morning cereal,
(more of it out than in the two year old).
He does not see me, and I watch him bend,
catnapping, overalled in limp content.
The toys I brought will wait until he mends.
"No sweets for Gregory," his daddy warned.
"Don't bring him candy, Mom. Bad for the teeth."
I think back to your baby days, my son.
A lollypop could always stop your tears.
The little monarch yawns himself awake;
shrieks with a child's unique display of joy
as I sit close to him. The oatmealed smile,
small hands that touch all features of my face
invite the eyes to mist at royal gifts
spontaneously given me to keep.

Edith Warner

Grandmothers Are Special

Grandmothers are giving as much as they are getting in their contacts with the young. Parents are not enough. For a child to have a full emotional life he needs some extra adults who love him and are to be trusted. This additional measure of essential affection a grandparent or two can supply.

Grandmothers do more than supplement parental affection and teaching. They complement it as well, for they extend the circle of important figures in a child's life. A child feels more at home in a world which he knows includes grownups besides Mother and Father who can and will take care of him, who like him as he is, and love him even though at the moment they might be speaking sternly to him.

Complementing the part that parents play, for many grandmothers, means being more tolerant of childish nonsense, noise and dirt than a harassed mother is. Not being on the job three hundred and sixty-five days a year makes it possible to enjoy nursery babble or teen talk, to take time to explain what life was like before there was television or watch the clouds turn pink in a sunset to the accompaniment of five-year-old wonder. She who grows weary knows she can rest tomorrow.

Edith G. Neisser

Pledge To A First Grandchild

Child of my child, of the man, my son
whom I sheltered long ago
helpless like you, O newborn one:
Now I shall watch you grow
until you, too, will walk alone,
unfettered into the world,
forging your way to a love of your own...
Today I feel you curled
into my arms, sweet limbs that yield
to the pledge in my first caress:
I shall not hold you as a shield
against my loneliness.

Anne Marx

Breakfast at Grandmother's house takes on a new meaning when that grandmother is "Baba." Join Janet Gillespie as she describes that special event.

Breakfast at Synton was no mere meal but a festival to celebrate the birth of a new day. It also had about it the glamour of a royal levee, and in summer we took turns attending. As the eldest I had the first day. Breakfast took place at exactly 8 o'clock and not one moment sooner, for Baba's routine was that of a lady of leisure in a Scottish country house during the reign of the late Queen Victoria.

I don't know how she did it, but Baba had the gift of turning the most commonplace event into a drama. A good example of this art was the morning flower ritual, when she selected (or was given) a perfect blossom to wear in her amethyst pin. In June I was supposed to procure a special symbolic flower—the purple milkwort—the herald of summer's beginning, as goldenrod was a symbol of its ending.

On that first morning Rajah, the peacock, woke me at sunrise. It was his custom every morning to fly up on the carriage-house roof and shriek like a madwoman. The sun was just coming over Synton at the top of the hill. Outside the front door the morning fizzed and glittered like a shaken ginger-ale bottle, bird song bubbled up through wet leaves, and the whole hill was scented with honeysuckle and freshly opened wild roses.

I went up the path between bushes of wet sweet fern

searching for the polygala. Across the path the wheels of the night's spider webs broke stickily against my face; I crawled under the best ones, and after a while I found one opened sprig of the sacred flower and ran the rest of the way out of sheer joy.

Baba stood with her head cocked slightly like a small hawk while I presented my flower.

"Ah, my polygala, the first of the summer," she said, threading it behind her amethyst.

"Dear Jan, you never forget. Now, I have a little treat for you!" She flung out her hand toward my place, where the first sweet peas stood in a bud vase. One was pale pink, the other violet. The centerpiece was an arrangement of old-fashioned roses, and Baba called off their names: moss rose, cabbage, damask, old French. "All very old," she said, "and with the true rose scent. Modern tea roses are nearly scentless," she added sternly. Baba took as much trouble arranging flowers for me as she would have for the King of England; she entertained her family as though they were honored guests. The table was set with the best silver and glass, and today we had the blue Canton china and an array of Japanese and Chinese jars containing Baba's preserves and jams and various imported honeys and marmalades.

"Always use the best of everything every day," Baba said often. "Who is more important than one's own family and oneself?"

When the French clock on the mantel struck eight in its clear silver voice, the kitchen clock whirred out the hour, and instantly Tink came through from the pantry, followed by Aunt K., carrying the oatmeal smoking in yellow bowls.

We all sat down. I sat opposite Tink, facing the conservatory, where the sun was shining through a jungle of green leaves.

Tink and I said grace.

"Thank you, God, for daily bread."

Then Baba looked up smiling and began the oatmeal

rites, which started with cream. This was placed in front of her in a squatty white pitcher with mayflowers on it. She poured off the thick yellow top cream onto her own cereal and said as she did so, "The cream of the jest." Then she passed me the pitcher, now containing bluish skim milk. This little foible made Baba human even as we ourselves. After all, people have to have *some* weakness. However, sugar was out of the question. Baba didn't intend to turn breakfast into a Babylonian orgy.

After the oatmeal there was the rite of the boiled eggs, which came to the table in the small end of blue willow egg cups wearing tiny cozies that Baba had made from the crimson silk of an Indian sari.

As breakfast drew to a close and Tink and I were each attempting to cram in one more hot biscuit with honey, the sound of steps on the porch heralded the daily procession of family. Hard shoes meant Mum; heavy, sneakered thuds, Pop; and light scampering sneakers the smaller members of the herd. After each one the screen door whirred shut and they came in out of the sun and the linden perfume to perch on a chair near the table.

Ancestry

Father's father's great-great-grandfather
*   Married his green-eyed scatter-brained love.*
How the townsfolk flared like a fanned pother!
*   What could he be thinking of?*

She was beautiful, mouth like a strawberry,
*   Hair the color of waving grain,*
Cheeks as soft as the bloom of hawberry,
*   Eyes as green as the pines of Maine.*

Children's children from them descendent,
*   Scribble verses or gaze at a cloud,*
Eyes reflecting the green resplendent
*   Fire of a scatter-brain, wild and proud.*

Eleanor Vinton

All In The Point Of View

At 44, I am about to become a grandmother. How thrilling it will be to be young enough to enjoy my grandchild, to be his friend and be able to enjoy the things he enjoys.

I feel sure that grandmothers in general aren't as old as they used to be. I remember my own gray-haired grandma—she'd have abhorred a dye job. We children loved her enormously, but we didn't think of her as fun. Then there was my own mother—grandma in her turn. She spoiled our youngsters, rocked and sang to them and humored their every notion. How patiently I taught them to respect her age and save her strength by running errands for her.

Being an elderly grandparent must be a rewarding experience that helps fill the long, inactive years. But I'm glad my grandchildren will have a young grandmother to remember.

Excuse me a minute—here comes my seven-year-old son with question marks in his eyes. What did you say, dear? Will I still be alive when you get married?

Well, goodbye, folks. This is where I came in.

Mary Ruth Duling

Turnabout

In Grandma's kitchen, after Sunday church,
The huge old oven warmly browned its pies,
As reverently Grandma'd pat the dough and perch
Her light bread on a window sill to rise.
Translucent glasses spoke of hilltop berries;
The milk would cool, the chicken pop and sing,
And eagerly I'd climb the dictionaries
To slip the napkin from its silver ring.
Now Grandma's first to notice and applaud
My paper napkins or new mats of plastic,
While heaps of golden drumsticks lately thawed
Find her, each Sunday, more enthusiastic.
And twinkling eyes acclaim a bright granddaughter
Whose angel food springs magically from water.

Alice Boyd Stockdale

The Jolly Pretense

On Halloween, the children come
In weird and witchy dress,
With ugly masks to hide their looks—
Most fearfull I confess—

And shopping bags they hope to fill
With goodies they amass,
To trade them in the days to come
With other kids in class.

One loaded sack I recognize
Is carried by a troll,
And when he tells me, "Trick or treat!"
My smile I pigeon-hole.

I offer him some lollipops,
He asks me first, "How many?"
And keeps pretending as I do
He doesn't know I'm Granny.

Jaye Giammarino

Grandma's Day

My grandma takes her shower
   At the very crack of dawn,
And she never fails to fix her hair
   Or put her makeup on.
Then she drives down on the freeway
   In a bright blue Thunderbird,
To a building called a courthouse,
   Where she has the final word.
When the bailiff sees her coming,
   He gives the clerk a nudge,
'Cause you see, my grandma truly is
   A most superior judge.

But when the sun is going down,
   And court's at last adjourned,
My grandma has a slew of things
   With which she's most concerned.
Sometimes she bakes an apple pie.
   Sometimes she frosts a cake.
When she does that, I lick the bowl—
   That is, if I'm awake.
But the nicest part of Grandma's day,
   Is when the lights are dim,
And she comes tip-toe up the stairs
   To see that I'm tucked in.

Lee Sobelman

What Grandparents Can Give

Our grandchildren in second grade read faster than we did in fifth grade; they do math in a new way that we can't understand; they get facts from television as fast as we get them. In none of these areas can we be of help. But helping them to understand that a brother, sister, playmate, parent, and even a grandparent sees things in a way that is totally different from the way they see it, is one way in which we can contribute. It is in small ways like this that we can be of help, we believe. Certainly, we have a lot of fun trying.

Jean Kinney

The Waiting Game

I knew when he first arrived in town.
   I heard the news on good authority,
   and though I couldn't wait to see him,
   I understood he had much business
   to attend to.

I filled the time with preparations
   for a festive homecoming.
   I made his bed with a new coverlet,
   arranged red roses for his bureau,
   and bought a record guaranteed
   to bring sweet dreams.

He is coming within the hour!
   I rearrange the coverlet and the roses,
   turn down the phonograph to low,
   look out the window and wonder once again
   how he will look when he arrives.
   Will he mind the cold rain falling?—
   (He's been so used to a warm climate.)

A horn is honking! The waiting is over!
   I open the door and my arms
   to my first grandchild.

Dorothy Joslin

Grandma Helps With The New Baby

It all brings back the days when her own children were around two, four, and six. She wonders now how on earth she ever managed then, how she ever got enough sleep. Did she jump during the night to see whether they were all covered? Did six o'clock seem early for her to start the day? And was she not thankful that it was not five when the children began to stir! Yes, she did it all in those other days. But somehow it is just a little bit different, now.

Yet Grandmother certainly felt it was a privilege to prepare the children for the coming of the new baby. They each made a little something for him, and Grandma gave her full time to making them happy away from their own home. She kept reminding them what the homecoming would be like, when there would be a real live baby, not just a doll, in the crib that they had left all ready for the big event.

At last the phone rang, and the good news came over the wire. It was a big bouncing boy! They danced and they sang, and ran around the living room to celebrate. "When can we go and see him? When?" That was the cry from then on. The day finally came when the phone rang again, and they were told that it was all right for the children to come home now. All was in readiness for them.

Now it was time to start for home. The children were as good as gold, but terribly excited. They stopped in front of the house, and all jumped out. There was Mom standing at the door, holding little brother all wrapped up in her arms. They were somewhat shy and held back a bit. But when Mom walked into the house carrying the baby, they all scampered in after her.

Grandpa said, "Now all sit down in a row on the sofa." They did, and Mom carefully placed the baby into each pair of arms extended to take him. Half a minute was plenty long enough! Then Grandpa put a new little toy he had bought for them into each child's lap. They were as happy as could be. The oldest one said to Grandma, "Grandma, did you ever see such a tiny baby? He was so little. I want to look at him again." By now the baby was in his crib, where his big brother felt such a tiny creature belonged.

In the meantime, Grandma had slipped unobtrusively into the kitchen, and had started to prepare lunch. She had to swallow a lump in her throat as she went about her task, for the little family scene had touched her deeply. She looked at Grandpa, standing in silence near his daughter. She could tell by his expression that he was thinking the same thoughts that she had.

Frank Howard Richardson

A Grandmother Is For Wondering

"Grandma, why isn't milk green?"

Reasonable question under the circumstances.

We were visiting my sister in Wisconsin. She and her husband had a big dairy herd. This was the first of many visits and were they ever a sight about sundown in the pasture. Black and white Holstein. Deep green grass. Lush. Then we watched the milking process done by machine. Next we went to their little creamery. Here the fascinating separator did its thing. Out of this spout, milk. Out of that, cream.

Grandma was with us. Since she was one of our favorite people, she often went where we went.

Suddenly at dinner, a question. Holding his big glass of pure white milk, he turned and said, "Grandma, why isn't milk green?"

So why isn't it?

Of course, he would ask grandma. Grandparents are for wondering. For wondering with, wondering about, just wondering.

A grandparent is for awe. For speculating on things nobody ever thought **before**.

Charlie W. Shedd

Amy Elizabeth Ermyntrude Annie

Amy Elizabeth Ermyntrude Annie
Went to the country to visit her Grannie.

Learnt to churn butter and learnt to make cheese,
Learnt to milk cows and take honey from bees.

Learnt to spice rose leaves and learnt to cure ham,
Learnt to make cider and black currant jam.

When she came home she could not settle down,
Said there was nothing to do in the town.

Nothing to do there and nothing to see:
Life was all shopping and afternoon tea.

Amy Elizabeth Ermyntrude Annie
Ran away back to the country and Grannie.

Queenie Scott Hopper

Britain's Queen Mother, now a great-grandmother, kept her grandchildren amused by constantly adding new tricks and games to her repertoire. The result was a lot of fun for the grandchildren—and for the grandmother!

The Queen Mother was once asked if she was not perhaps inclined to spoil her grandchildren.

"But of course," she replied. "Spoiling your grandchildren is half the fun of being a grandmother."

Where her grandchildren were concerned, nothing was—or is now, for that matter—too much trouble for her. Gifted with infinite patience and the ability to get down to the level of childhood without any sense of condescension, she loved having them around her . . . and they loved being with her. At this stage of their lives, she played games such as ludo and snakes-and-ladders with them as well as joining them in more active pastimes such as hide-and-seek. She taught them to play patience, a card game with which she often whiles away a leisure hour.

Mastery of a few simple conjuring tricks made her, in the eyes of her grandchildren, only a shade less remarkable than the fairy godmother in a pantomime. A favourite trick was one in which she seemed to pass pennies right through her hand so that, empty at the outset, it was suddenly and mystifyingly full of coins. Of course, the children were not completely satisfied until they too knew how it was done.

"I really must learn some more tricks," the Queen Mother confided in a friend. "I simply cannot keep pace with the demand."

Graham and Heather Fisher

Just Happen To Have Some Pictures

May heaven help me not to tell
The things my grandchildren do well!
And may I never once relate
The darling words the children prate,
Or show their photographs or brag
on them . . . unless the others drag
Their own grandchildren's pictures out
And then, so help me, I must spout!

Nova Trimble Ashley

Granny Grows Younger

Just as childhood emerged in the fifteenth century, adolescence at the beginning of the twentieth, and youth at midcentury, so, too, has a new generation of women—products of medical technology—appeared on the scene today. These women do not fit any of the old stereotypes. They announce, with as much surprise and incredulity as they expect to find in their listeners, that they are *grand*mothers! And in the near future they will be *great*-grandmothers, for the four-generation family is almost inevitable.

Traditionally the image of the grandmother has been one of a benign little old lady delightedly serving roast turkey and pumpkin pie to a large family. It has now become common to speak of glamorous grandmothers. As, indeed, many of them, still only in their late forties or fifties, are.

Jessie Bernard

Walking With Grandma

I like to walk with Grandma;
Her steps are short like mine.
She doesn't say, "Now hurry up,"
She always takes her time.

I like to walk with Grandma;
Her eyes see things mine do—
Wee pebbles bright, a funny cloud,
Half-hidden drops of dew.

Most people have to hurry;
They do not stop and see.
I'm glad that God made Grandmas
Unrushed and young like me!

Mildred R. Grenier

So Long As We Love

So long as we love we serve; so long as we are loved by others, I would almost say we are indispensable. The true services of life are inestimable in money, and are never paid. Kind words and caresses, high and wise thoughts, humane designs, tender behaviour to the weak and suffering, and all the charities of man's existence, are neither bought nor sold.

Robert Louis Stevenson

Generations

At an age when many women are great-grandmothers, the anthropologist Margaret Mead became a grandmother for the first time when her daughter, Catherine, gave birth to a baby girl. Though she had spent a great portion of her life studying motherhood in primitive cultures, one aspect of her own experience came as a complete surprise. "I suddenly realized," she writes in the autobiographical *Blackberry Winter,* "that through no act of my own I had become biologically related to a new human being."

From the time of her childhood, she says, she had been able to conceive of her relationship with all of her forebears. "But the idea that as a grandparent one was dealing with action at a distance—that somewhere, miles away, a series of events occurred that changed one's own status forever—I had not thought of that and I found it very odd. . . .

"Scientists and philosophers have speculated at length about the sources of man's belief that he is a creature with a future life . . . Speculation may be the only kind of answer that is possible, but I would now add to the speculations that are more familiar another of my own: the extraordinary sense of having been transformed not by any act of one's own but by the act of one's child."

Ruth Goode

Old Log House

On a little green knoll
At the edge of the wood
My great great grandmother's
First house stood.

The house was of logs
My grandmother said
With one big room
And a lean-to shed.

The logs were cut
And the house was raised
By pioneer men
In the olden days.

I like to hear
My grandmother tell
How they built the fireplace
And dug the well.

They split the shingles;
They filled each chink,
It's a house of which
I like to think.

Forever and ever
I wish I could
Live in a house
At the edge of a wood.

James S. Tippett

Barter

Life has loveliness to sell,
    All beautiful and splendid things,
Blue waves whitened on a cliff,
    Soaring fire that sways and sings,
And children's faces looking up
Holding wonder like a cup.

Life has loveliness to sell,
    Music like a curve of gold,
Scent of pine trees in the rain,
    Eyes that love you, arms that hold,
And for your spirit's still delight,
Holy thoughts that star the night.

Spend all you have for loveliness,
    Buy it and never count the cost;
For one white singing hour of peace
    Count many a year of strife well lost,
And for a breath of ecstasy
Give all you have been, or could be.

Sara Teasdale

Less Is More

One cannot collect all the beautiful shells on the beach. One can collect only a few, and they are more beautiful if they are few. One moon shell is more impressive than three. There is only one moon in the sky. One double-sunrise is an event; six are a succession, like a week of schooldays. Gradually one discards and keeps just the perfect specimen; not necessarily a rare shell, but a perfect one of its kind. One sets it apart by itself, ringed around by space—like the island.

For it is only framed in space that beauty blooms. Only in space are events and objects and people unique and significant—and therefore beautiful. A tree has significance if one sees it against the empty face of sky. A note in music gains significance from the silences on either side. A candle flowers in the space of night. Even small and casual things take on significance if they are washed in space, like a few autumn grasses in one corner of an Oriental painting, the rest of the page bare.

Anne Morrow Lindbergh

Glimpses

A moment ago
I saw a leaf,
Or was it a bird?
A glimpse so brief
Fails entirely
To tell the eye
The truth of things
That sail the sky.
A glimpse so brief
Of bird or love
Is not enough for a mind possessed.
Intellect thinks itself bereft
When only wonderment is left.

Patricia Hubbell

Color

Oh, God, how grateful we all should be for color.

For blue skies and blue eyes and this little blue dress that I'm hanging on the line.

For oranges vivid in the brown basket that sits upon my kitchen table. For the purple grapes that choke the fence, and the lavender cups of morning glories against a white garage.

What a lovely thing—the interplay of colors in a paisley blouse. A throw rug. A bracelet. A vase on the shelf. I think of all the unsung artists and craftsmen who have produced them, and the marvelous routes and ways of trade and commerce that must weave and interplay— like the intermingling colors—to bring them all into my home to enrich and heighten the pattern of all our lives.

I am grateful, God, for all red things. For cannas, and scarlet cardinals. For the ruby red of cherries. The red on a woodpecker's throat. The bright living red of my own blood flowing. And the faded red of old boxcars or wind-beaten barns.

I offer up thanks, dear God, for green. That leaves are green of countless shades—and so are the grasses and growths with which you've chosen to carpet your world. And that we, your people, are given gifts that enable us to copy those limitless greens in paint and fabrics, in wall-papers and leathers and dyes.

I am happy, Lord, for yellow. The golden yellow of sunshine, and butter, and daffodils, and autumn trees. For the lovely yellow—so rich, so intense—in an egg yolk, a lemon, a length of ribbon, a pair of bright new shoes.

And you gather up all these many colors into an arch of misty ribbons and turn them into a rainbow for our delight. As if the whole beautiful earth were being packaged up and tied with a bow.

How grateful we should be that you didn't give us a drab, sere world, or one in mere black and white. That you decided to make even people in so many shades of skin and hair and eyes. How dull it would be, Lord, if all races and all faces looked alike.

Thank you, God, for color. All the exciting hues that drench the earth and stir the senses. And for giving us the eyes with which to see them. Thank you, God, for the miracle of sight.

Marjorie Holmes

On Wings More Delicate

The butterflies go fluttering by.
How do they know that they can fly?
Had we been only crawling things,
Would we know what to do with wings?
I wonder. Still I think we might,
For we too have our hopes of flight,
Though of a different kind
Since ours is mainly in our mind.
We have to trust ourselves on less
Than even air or emptiness
On wings more delicately wrought
Than butterflies—mere wings of thought—
But oh, sometimes with what surprise
How exquisitely high we rise!

James Dillet Freeman

Out Of The Leaf-Falls

These are the things to cherish:
  A seed and a dream and a child;
Else must the nations perish,
  And earth fall away to the wild.
These are the things to nourish:
  The budding of trees and youth;
So shall the grown things flourish—
  Manhood and beauty and truth.
Out of the leaf-falls that perish,
  Retrieved from the waste and the wild,
These are the things to cherish:
  A seed and a dream and a child.

Author Unknown

Each Day's Gift

The man of the house brought me in a bright but somewhat stunted little gladiolus bloom a few days ago. I was delighted. Then, as I arranged it with some greenery in a decorative vase, I smiled to think how I would have spurned this flower a few short weeks ago.

In midsummer the gladioli were in full bloom, so heavy that they bent on the sturdy stalks, and as each blossom opened, the color climbed the spearlike stem to its uppermost tip. They were large blossoms with velvety petals, shades ranging from a white so pure it seemed like morning snow in winter to red so deep it seemed like blood. Wide bowls and tall containers were required to display the bounty of their loveliness.

But now it is autumn; the foliage of the flowers we picked earlier is turning brown and dry. When a sudden bonus appears and a flower shows up among this dying, withering process, we feel especially appreciative. So I welcome the bloom I would have cast aside in another season.

The same is true of our vegetables. When tomatoes were at their peak, we sliced only the largest, ripest, most perfect specimens for our table. And Golden Bantam corn had to be at just the right moment of ripeness, fullness,

milkiness for us to pick it. Now we handle knobby little tomatoes with care and lay them on the kitchen window sill
to grow a little redder. Nubbins of corn we would have
overlooked on an earlier day are welcome tidbits, a last
link with summer's abundance.

As we scavenge for the last fruits of summer and enjoy
some of the final remnants as much as—perhaps more
than—we did the first harvest, I wonder if we do this in
our living, too. In the wealth of time which surrounds us
when we are children we can be prodigal with hours and
days. Then as the years begin to shorten, we grow more
aware of the briefness of our days and we begin to savor
the seconds and the minutes. Weeks we once might have
dribbled away to little purpose now seem as precious as a
month did then. Nubbins of time are suddenly sweeter than
the full grain of seasons once taken for granted.

I look at my last glad blossom of the year and I enjoy
it because it was unexpected. I relish the sweetness of the
last sun-ripened tomato because it was a volunteer. Who
knows what may flower in what corner in what season—if
we look to each day's gift?

Wilma Dykeman

Counters

To think I once saw grocery shops
    With but a casual eye
And fingered figs and apricots
    As one who came to buy!

To think I never dreamed of how
    Bananas swayed in rain,
And often looked at oranges
    Yet never thought of Spain!

And in those wasted days I saw
    No sails about the tea—
For grocery shops were grocery shops,
    Not hemispheres to me!

Elizabeth Coatsworth

Grandma Moses—Farmwife Into Legend

Of all forms of starting, starting late is probably the most fulfilling and liberating. It comes for most of those who do accomplish their aims as the icing on the cake—the dessert they have been longing for all their lives. Starting late is a risk, like all starting, but the older one becomes, the more one recognizes that all life is a risk. Why not throw it all on a chance to win? What *is* there left to lose after all? Most of us go through life with a minimum of individual courage, following the curve of what is expected, accepting a prepackaged form to our lives; copying, like an example in a book, the personas of those who have met society's standards, while we by-pass the person we should like to become. Those who break out of this mold, in the late years of their lives, are a special breed.

Grandma Moses is probably the most famous late starter in our history. For those who moan about what they've put off doing, her story has been the great American consoling myth to persuade them that it's never too late to start. It can't fail to appeal—a startling flight, from nonentity to world-famous painter, accomplished by a quaint little farm woman well over the age of seventy, as real as the soil from which she sprang.

Working, keeping busy was Mary Robertson Moses's life. Bringing in a little extra cash was always a useful thing to do. Giving pleasure was a joy. She did so with whatever came to hand—making cookies, jams, rugs, yarn pictures, quilts, dolls, and finally, when arthritis made it too painful to pursue fine handwork, with the oil paintings she had begun to do, just for the fun. The "dabbling in oil" she refers to in her autobiography evokes an artist's palette, tubes of paint, studio light. Nothing of the sort. House paint, a single lightbulb, her work table "an old-fashioned contraption with panels on four sides" decorated all over with landscapes painted when Grandma Moses was approximately fifty-five, to pretty up the table.

The New York City department store Gimbels sponsored her second one-man show and brought Grandma Moses down to New York for it. It was held in a huge hall which overwhelmed the modestly small paintings and where a tremendous crowd, mainly women, overwhelmed the tiny woman, as well. Grandma, led to a microphone to make a speech about art, seemed to become disoriented, looking about wonderingly at her alien audience. There was a long, uncomfortable pause and then she told the well-dressed audience of women how she made her preserves, and how good they were, and she produced a few small jars out of her handbag and offered them as samples.

If she could not articulate an expressive esthetic of painting, nevertheless she knew what she was about. She kept meticulously true to the scenes of the beautiful valleys where she had lived out her hard-working life, the Shenandoah, and the charmingly varied landscape of towns, valley, mountains, and falling streams of the New York-Vermont border country. The new paintings she produced in her last years re-stated the old simplicities in the luminous colors she loved. She used glitter on her winter landscapes. To some artistic adviser who tried to dissuade her from this practice she stubbornly insisted that they could not have properly looked at the country landscape on a sunny winter's day. "To me there is no winter landscape without the sparkle on the snow!" She went on painting into her nineties, incredibly with more assurance and artistic discretion. The Oriental delicacy of composition once noted by the late writer and art collector, Louis Bromfield, is most striking in these last works. When asked, she offered her recipe for doing art with the same straightforwardness she would have responded to a request for a recipe for preserving raspberries.

"Some one has asked how I paint and what on. Well I like masonite tempered presd wood, the harder the better. I prefer it to canvas, as it will last longer. I go over this with linseed oil, then with three coats of flat white paint, now I saw it to fit the Frames . . ."

She died in 1960 at the age of one hundred, having produced more than a thousand paintings of fair size and perhaps half as many postcard size. She was world-famous. The little old farm woman from Hoosick Falls, who ended her autobiography with the words "Now this is to give you an idea of who and what I am . . ." had certainly fulfilled her intent.

Helen Yglesias

A Blackbird Suddenly

Heaven is in my hand, and I
Touch a heart-beat of the sky,
Hearing a blackbird's cry.

Strange, beautiful, unquiet thing,
Lone flute of God, how can you sing
Winter to spring?

Joseph Auslander

Keep Still

Look, and keep very still,
Still as a tree,
And if you do you will
Presently see
The doe come down to drink
Leading her fawn
Just as they did, I think,
In the first dawn.

Eleanor Farjeon

A Wonderful Age

Today I have completed sixty-four Springtimes...And now here I am, a very old woman, embarked on my sixty-fifth year. By one of those strange oddities in my destiny, I am now in much better health, much stronger, much more active, than I ever was in my youth....I am troubled by no hankering after the days of my youth: I am no longer ambitious for fame: I desire no money except insofar as I should like to be able to leave something to my children and grandchildren....This astonishing old age...has brought me neither infirmity nor lowered vitality.

Can I still make myself useful? That one may legitimately ask, and I think that I can answer 'yes.' I feel that I may be useful in a more personal, more direct way than ever before. I have, though how I do not know, acquired much wisdom. I am better equipped to bring up children....It is quite wrong to think of old age as a downward slope. One climbs higher and higher with the advancing years, and that, too, with surprising strides.

How good life is when all that one loves is aswarm with life!

George Sand

More Than I Hoped For

My grandson Marshall is helping to conduct a university survey of senior citizens, and has asked me to fill in a questionnaire.

Some of the questions I shall simply ignore, but the following one made me sit up and think:

Have you accomplished as much as you had hoped you would?

I decided that my answer would be, "more," because I realized that when I was a young woman I was mainly concerned with my husband, my home, and looking after my children.

It was much later that I discovered a new world of volunteer work at my church, and for my community. After my husband died I took a job which further broadened my horizon.

These may not be great accomplishments, but each one of them has deepened my understanding of people. Yes, I have accomplished more than I had hoped for, as my life has become fuller and richer than I ever expected it to be.

Edna McCann

The Coin

Into my heart's treasury
I slipped a coin
That time cannot take
Nor thief purloin, —
Oh, better than the minting
Of a gold-crowned king
Is the safe-kept memory
Of a lovely thing.

Sara Teasdale

Designed by Bob Pantelone
Illustrated by Kay Bedard Ohlson
Type set in Garamond

Acknowledgments

The editor and the publisher have made every effort to trace the ownership of all copyrighted material and to secure permission from copyright holders of such material. In the event of any question arising as to the use of any material the publisher and editor, while expressing regret for inadvertent error, will be pleased to make the necessary corrections in future printings. Thanks are due to the following authors, publishers, publications and agents for permission to use the material indicated.

ATHENEUM PUBLISHERS, INC., for "Glimpses" from *Catch Me a Wind* by Patricia Hubbell. Copyright © 1968 by Patricia Hubbell.

WILLIAM L. BAUHAN, PUBLISHER, for "Ancestry" from *On The Contoocook* by Eleanor Vinton. Copyright © 1974 by Eleanor Vinton.

COLLIER-MACMILLAN CANADA LTD., for an excerpt from *The Heritage Book*. Copyright © 1978 by Edna McCann.

COWARD, McCANN & GOEGHEGAN, INC., for "Counters" from *Compass Rose* by Elizabeth Coatsworth. Copyright © 1929 by Coward-McCann, Inc., renewed 1957 by Elizabeth Coatsworth.

DAILY WORD, for "On Wings More Delicate" by James Dillet Freeman from April 1979 issue of *Daily Word*.

THE DIAL PRESS, for an excerpt from *The Future of Motherhood* by Jessie Bernard. Copyright © 1974 by Jessie Bernard.

DOUBLEDAY & COMPANY, INC., for an excerpt from *Penny Candy* by Jean Kerr. Copyright © 1966, 1967, 1968, 1969, 1970 by Collin Productions, Inc.; for an excerpt from *Grandparents* by Charlie W. Shedd. Copyright © 1976 by Charlie W. Shedd and The Abundance Foundation.

ELSEVIER/NELSON BOOKS, for an excerpt from *Living With Zest in an Empty Nest* by Jean Kinney. Copyright © 1970 by Jean Kinney; for an excerpt from *Prince Charles: The Future King* by Graham and Heather Fisher. Copyright © 1967 by Graham and Heather Fisher.

M. EVANS AND COMPANY, INC., for an excerpt from *Getting Along With Your Grown-Up Children* by Helene S. Arnstein. Copyright © 1970 by Helene S. Arnstein.

FARM JOURNAL, INC., for "All in a Point of View" by Mary Ruth Duling and "Turnabout" by Alice Stockdale, from Farm Journal's *This Way of Life*. Copyright © 1971 by Farm Journal, Inc. Reprinted by special permission of publisher.

JOSLIN, DOROTHY, for "To My Grandson, Alexander." Copyright © 1978 by Dorothy Joslin and "The Waiting Game." Copyright © 1972 by Dorothy Joslin.

HARPER & ROW, PUBLISHERS, INC., for an excerpt from *Mothers and Daughters* by Edith G. Neisser. Copyright © 1967 by Edith G. Neisser; for excerpts from *A Joyful Noise* by Janet Gillespie. Copyright © 1971 by Janet Gillespie; for an excerpt from *Lelia: The Life of George Sand* by Andre Maurois. Copyright © 1953 by Andre Maurois; for "The Old Log House" from *A World to Know* by James S. Tippett. Copyright © 1933 by Harper & Row, Publishers, Inc., renewed 1961 by Martha K. Tippett; for "A Blackbird Suddenly" from *Sunrise Trumpets* by Joseph Auslander. Copyright © 1924 by Harper & Row, Publishers, Inc., renewed 1952 by Joseph Auslander.

HOLMES, MARJORIE AND TONI MENDEZ, INC., for "Color" from *I've Got to Talk to Somebody, God* by Marjorie Holmes. Copyright © 1968, 1969, 1971 by Marjorie Holmes Mighell.

HOLT, RINEHART AND WINSTON, for an excerpt from *Look to This Day* by Wilma Dykeman. Copyright © 1968 by Wilma Dykeman Stokely.

J. P. LIPPINCOTT, PUBLISHERS, for "Keep Still" from *Eleanor Farjeon's Poems For Children*. (Originally appeared in *Over the Garden Wall* by Eleanor Farjeon.) Copyright © 1933, 1961, by Eleanor Farjeon.

LITTLE, BROWN AND COMPANY, for "The Pushover" from *You Can't Get There From Here* by Ogden Nash. Copyright © 1956 by Ogden Nash.

MACMILLAN PUBLISHING CO., INC., for "Barter" from *Collected Poems* by Sara Teasdale. Copyright © 1917 by Macmillan Publishing Co., Inc., renewed 1945 by Mamie T. Whelass; for "The Coin" from *Collected Poems* by Sara Teasdale. Copyright © 1920 by Macmillan Publishing Co., Inc., renewed 1948 by Mamie T. Whelass; for "An Unplanned Visit" from *A Book for Grandmothers* by Ruth Goode. Copyright © 1976 by Ruth Goode.

DAVID McKAY COMPANY, INC., for an excerpt from *Grandparents and Their Families* by Frank Howard Richardson, M.D. Copyright © 1964 by Frank Howard Richardson, M.D.

MARX, ANNE AND THE GOLDEN QUILL PRESS, for "Small Fortune" (originally appeared in *Good Housekeeping*) and "Pledge to a First Grandchild" from *By Way of Life*. Copyright © 1970 by Anne Marx.

MODERN MATURITY, for an excerpt by Jaye Giammarino from October-November 1974 issue of *Modern Maturity*. Copyright © 1972 (1977) by The American Association of Retired Persons.

WILLIAM MORROW & COMPANY, INC., for an excerpt in *The Mother Book* by Liz Smith from *Blackberry Winter* by Margaret Mead. Copyright © 1972 by Margaret Mead.

THE NATIONAL LEAGUE OF PEN WOMEN, for "A Child Ran Here" by Elizabeth Revere from the October 1977 issue of *The Pen Woman*; for "The Little Monarch" by Edith Warner from the May 1979 issue of *The Pen Woman*.

PANTHEON BOOKS, A DIVISION OF RANDOM HOUSE, INC., for an excerpt from *Gift From The Sea* by Anne Morrow Lindbergh. Copyright © 1955 by Anne Morrow Lindbergh.

RAWSON, WADE PUBLISHERS, INC., for an excerpt from *Starting Early, Anew, Over and Late* by Helen Yglesias. Copyright © 1978 by Helen Yglesias.

THE UNITED METHODIST PUBLISHING HOUSE, for "Walking With Grandma" by Mildred R. Grenier. Reprinted from April, 1959 issue of *Together*. Copyright © 1959 by Lovich Pierce Inc.

THE VIKING PRESS, (VIKING PENGUIN INC.) for "About Children" from *Times Three* by Phyllis McGinley. Copyright © 1951 by Phyllis McGinley, renewed 1979 by Julie Elizabeth and Phyllis H. Blake. (Originally appeared in *The New Yorker*.)